Gutpunched by Love or at Least,

Something

# Gutpunched by Love or at Least, Something

Joe Currie

Clockwork Fox Press

for a world full of people in pain, ones with stronger resolve
than me that fight to make it better.

**- Compost**

Once your life
has turned to shit
know the best flowers
can grow from it.

## - Leftover Love

I see you still,
sometimes,
in the slow curl
of a crocus petal.

How are you still
T R A M P L I N G
the mossgrown boneyards
inside my head?

Last orders
were called on us,
but you persist
like a boxer's fist.
A half-drowned maniac.
An evergreen pine.
        An echo.

This skull is no place for you now,
the home that we built here
has been abandoned by us both
to time
       to dust
          to the slow seasons
              to rust.

Only the foundations remain
but still,
       they remain.

## - Moths

flying through the night
with wings charcoaled
by self-immolation,
hoping that the light
will draw in someone
for us to love.

Dragged along moonlit
cracked-bone pavements
comes my heart,
grinning like a drunkard.
What has it found this time,
I wonder?
A sequinned face?
      A shell-curve body?
            A sunshine mind?

There is a goldfinch
hiding in the bushes,
laughing at this muscle's
throbbing stupidity.
It still insists on falling
for silk-lipped strangers
with a gasping violence,
even as it weeps
from all its plastered cracks.

You bite my lip
like the teeth of a saw
as the dawn vomits
over jackdaw skies.

We watch from the window and wonder:
where will these wisps of cloud end up
at the death of the day?

## - Circling the baggage reclaim

I have seen men
sobbing, drunk,
so far taken
from the everyday
and overwhelmed
with the relief of it.
I could never wander
so far into that hazy meadow,
into such a quiet abyss.
I carry too many things
that I refuse to put down.

There are signs telling me
not to leave my baggage unattended
and for once I am a good citizen.
And yes officer, I packed it myself,
and yes officer, I know the fabric is bloodstained,
but what am I meant to do
with these things that shrink
from any searchlight
exposing my shadows?

My broken back
will not belay my smile.
This heavy pack
is full of all the things
that have walked
            into rivers
                        with stone-weighted pockets
                                        on my watch.

**- Love, I have given you all and now I am nothing**

There's no more rain
in Big Heart Lake.
Its dried up now.
Go home.
        No swimming.

## - Well then, fuck.

And here I thought
you were another
choked up with the words.
With your heart still stuck
somewhere at the end of a sunset,
somewhere lit by a crematorium's flames.

I would have followed
the moonbeams that trail
from the curves of your skin.
I would have slept on a park bench
under a sky of long-dead stars
just to search for some comparison
to your watercolour eyes.

I will tell any who will listen
not to do what I have done.
Not to crack their ribcage,
to reveal their bruises to another.
Not to find themselves
asking that eternal question:
Was it worth the pain?
      Is it worth the pain?
          Is it worth the

               love?

## - The Climb

The darkness in my head
has begun to leak again,
slow and cacophonous
like soot-stained tears.

Isn't it funny how alone
you feel while in pain,
when really, you're a brick
in a towerblock of splintered bricks.

We are the bricks that hold up the world.
We, the still swinging underdogs,
    the lopsided smilers,
    the dirty shirt losers
stumbling at the back of this human race.

I have closed my eyes in a casual pain.
I have left knuckle prints on the walls
wishing each to be a knockout blow
to the faceless voices in my head.

I have been there,
    curled up at the bottom,
but I came back.
    And I'll come back.

I'll come back.

## - Lighthouses

Such a bright smile
wandering lost in the gloam,
just bright enough
to feel like a home,
with an open log fire
and a whisky for me,
sheltered from rain,
raised from the sea.

Our own coastal hide out,
our own carved out nook,
lying naked in bed
and reading a book.
We're warped like the floorboards,
the old, bow-backed joist,
but we're warped now together,
together, by choice.

## - Ribcage piano teeth play only classical tunes

There's melody in the still places
that only some ever hear.

Places where the wind skims
over endless, bowing heather.
The streets at early morning.
Your creekbed tearducts,
        anywhere underwater,
factories past close
with dust drifting to sleep
across the hum-quiet machines.

My ribs are an ivory fretboard.
Why is my heart bashing
them like a bass drum?

It wants to join in the music
that your love is singing

but I never taught it
        how to play.

**- Fighting back**

Scar pages with
the gentle smudges
of your words.
It is a small victory
against a world
that has scarred you so.

**- How can you love another when you're so full of hatred for yourself?**

What foreign architecture
supports your mind?
It is the bones of lost cities
rising from sands
in a desert storm.
It is a swollen chalice
spilling sunbeams
onto worn flagstones.

As I watched you leave
my clench-jawed brain questioned
how my heart can lie so well
without a mouth.

The albatross around my neck
tugs me forward, stumbl
                        ing
into pitfalls and rockslides,
like life has become a game
of snakes and snakes,
falling down the board
to: what?

Avoid the seething crowds.
Avoid the shine of bejewelled collars.

Walk the abandoned rail tracks,
the wind will echo whispers from the Gods
through the crumblestone tunnels
and blow embers
into your soul.

Only when you've loved yourself
will the world bow down.

**- The clouds rise from the horizon like the smoke of
wildfires.**

Some days the world is cold.
Some days sit on your chest
like a thrown fist.
We are ripped open
by what we cannot see,
ghostly hands tugging
at our fishgut souls
until they tear away.
The sun glares
at our shortcomings
but the moon
looks on with a lover's gaze.
Some days the world is cold.

Some days we die
and some days we don't.

## - Godot

There is an ache
in the bones
of each of us.

A slow yearning
for a sunset,

        or a Sunday,

           or *something*.

## - The best thing about being a wolf is the scared looks of all the sheep

How hard it is
not to scar yourself
when you lie in sawdust,
the vice tight
on your splintering ribs,
iron filings
drowning your lungs
and chest-pump mewling.

How to compare
that which scars
   and fades
with a pain that commits
   to neither

The words of your head
will rust into your bones.

The clouds move through the sky like Oxen.

The best thing about being a wolf
is the scared looks of all the sheep.

My scars crack
and purple in winter.
How gentle I must be with myself
when you are around.

The bags under my eyes
weigh down my face.

The carved-out hollows
of yours tell me
to sit on hilltops
in the sideways rain.

Sit on hilltops
and pretend you have rusted.

There is something
slowly draining from us.
Shall we sit
              and rust
                        together?

## - The weight of concrete

The landscape here
is monotoned grey,
like dirty snowmelt
slipped from clouds
and smothered
what it found below.

There is a reason
for everything here.

A reason for each
uniform piece
of machine,
but where I grew up
the fields were wildfires
of red and yellow.
Ivy crawled up brickwork
and young willows
and old oaks
were all green
for no reason at all.

### - Woman, reading.

The way you hold your paperback
is the way my bones ache,
and I could watch you, framed
by the bay windows
until those pale leaves grew autumnal.

The way you hold your paperback
is the way hairs stand up
on a moth's back like lightning,
rigid against the cream moonlight.

The way you hold your paperback
is the way a falcon brushes its wingtips
through the wide yawn of clouds
while the bones of Old Ones
make a promise of rain.

The way you hold your paperback
is the way some study tea leaves,
filled with a gutstab hope
that someone is scratching out
a good story for us all.

## - Polyfilla skull

There is a madman in my head
who they call BlackDog,
                    MadDog.

He is flailing wild
with hammer held hands,
cracking at this brittle-
bone, sorry-
                    shard skull.

How many hairline fractures
does it take to destroy a mind?

I coat the damage with filler,
spatula-smoothing the holes
circling round and round
in constant motion with this thing.
He doesn't stop,
so neither can I.

Unless I did.

Unless I let the starlit ocean
of his music
rip through the world,
shredding whatever it touched
with tears
and hook-knives,
chests bursting wounds,
wives waving frantic
with empty pill boxes,
doors bolted -

sunken-eyed inmates.

Is there laughter in rooms like this
or is it the gasping wind
whistling through the gaps
in tangled-wire minds?

I ask the question
but I don't want the answer.

I avoid eye contact
with whatever truths
curl tears and smiles
across the rippleglass
of our berry-sloe eyes.

## - Blood Trails

Imagine a world
where our wounds
didn't wrap their fists
so tight
around our hearts.

Where the rusted bones
sunken to seabeds
were raised from
the tangle of weeds.

Where the dragonsmog
of vaporous time
was chased by laughing children
into fields of carnivorous
heather.

**- The one with brighter eyes**

Do not cry
for the one
who mistook you
for anything less
than stardust.

Somewhere
there is another,
with brighter eyes,
who wants to
share your pain.
            dry your tears.
                    make you smile.
                            eat you out.

## - Underbite Piranhas

I find my mind crawling from a wreck.
Sleepless nights of catscream thoughts
stalking each other,
                circling each other,
like underbite piranhas at 3am.
The world is less than it once was.
The canned drone of a battleship
occurring only outside my curtains
and never where I am.

There is beauty
in the flowers
that punch their way
free of the ground.
And yet,
here we all are,
our nail-raked backs
frowning to the wasted petals,
watching the passing clouds
and searching for fingerprints
left by the Gods.

## - Cry and Divide

I have walked at night
and seen the smoke
that rises from drains.
The pale faces
pressed against window panes,
breathing out buried moments
stuck on repeat in tapedeck minds.

Maybe you'd go mad too,
if you lived in a head like this.
The world is little
but silhouettes in mist,
fractured memories
of those we've kissed
dancing like musicbox ballerinas
through the barrows of our thoughts.

So cry and divide,
        cry and divide.
Fall further back
into the ridges of your mind.
Try to guess the sum of your bones
laid out upon the warped floorboards
and pray you're not the last of your kind.

## - Five-day old Hibiscus

You hand me dried out flowers,
collapsing in the caress of the wind,
and hate me
        because I cannot make them bloom.

## - Lost and Found

Halfway in a dream,
waving woman, glasses,
a whole blackness -
the most intact thing I've known.
I was sitting in the classroom
but I was underwater,
splitting slow the roofbeams,
wrapped up in torpor
like mosquito amber,
suspended now in nothing
all I know, I know.
Cold and slow awakening,
lost and found at home.

## - The days are long and fold up like origami cranes

There's so many there;
maintaining motorcycles
in their oilslick driveways,
the wind playing kisschase
with their jackets and hair.
The ones with sandpaper hands,
capable of making something
of this fallen trunk world.

These creators,
the keys to their locks
t r e m b l e
like fingerbones
in a storm.

These ones turn the Earth
from sunrise to setting.
They are the artists,
    the watchers.
The introspective readers
    and exotic dancers.
They are the thinkers,
    and the doers.

They are you and me,
and all those
still on the streets
with Molotovs
mixing up souls.

But where are they now?

Tonight,
I am no longer sure
whether this world
still turns
toward morning.

## - Compass

There is a boy
in a photograph
somewhere under my bed
who knows
the Sun spins itself
over horizons
in ever tightening spheres,
east to west,
east to west.
He bruises roads at night,
headlights blazing sunrays,
heading west and east
and north,
        always north.

North is mythical.
It is layers and layers of snow
compacting themselves,
fossilising into bedsheets of ice.
The centre of the Earth
may be a roaring ball of fire
but the centre of The North
is a quiet inhalation
in a dark cave.

The boy longs for The North,
for unreachable places
with watercolour skies
and endless night.
He knows that the bubbles
that boil in his blood
would keep him warm.

I look at the boy
and he looks back.
The ice has invaded our eyes.
I wonder where he would have gone
if he'd known where we'd end up.

**- Some days the heroes of our hearts hold knives
unnoticed to our throats**

Stapled to bedsheets,
writing riddles
to this illness in the stars.
Some days the heroes of our hearts
hold knives unnoticed to our throats.

What is this fear
whose fingers
are wrapped so tight
around your ribcage?

One day
I broke myself,
and when I healed,
I healed crooked.
There are fractures
of old pains
slicing the flesh
of each of us,
cutting their way
from old photographs
to question when
the light left our eyes.

As sure as the birds
that flock from here
carve their way
to rhodonite skies,
there is more to read
in the gaps between words,

the negative space
that fills your lungs
but always leaves you
gasping for breath.

In truth, some days
I think I've figured out how to live,
but others I'm sure
there's just less of me left to kill.

**- A.G**

What fire there is
that burns within you,
such that sunflowers
would turn their heads.

## - Each day framed as a raindrop against a windowpane

There are days when the world
beyond the window sinks
like an insomniac's eyes.
Bruised, slaughtered and bled through,
greying beneath some mindfog.

Days when knives glimmer
from the washboard
with intense haste.
Days when the blood will not scrub clean.
The birds no longer exist,
they are all clipped
for having too much freedom.
Days that pass like sighs,
like slow-rolled eyes.

Days when the clouds do nothing but sneer,
when the motorways are backed up.
Days I'm convinced I cannot do this,
days I think *I cannot be here anymore.*

How many days have there been,
strung up on crosses like this?
So many days passing
between the sun's rotations.
Days that choose themselves
by throwing darts at a calendar.

Isn't it all
just a big
fucking
joke.

## - Don't let life question your worth

There is some magnetism,
pulling this room towards yours
across the dark street
with the hum-taxis
and callous streetlights.
This world is leaning
to the point of collapse,
aching its way to you
in some concave spiral.
These are shivering nights
drowning in pooled tears
from car headlights.
In the dimming light
I often wonder
if I'm worth saving,
but in the darkness
the steady beat:
I am

   I am

      I am.

**- Alone, arms linked, in rainfall at the end of a pier.**

It was two souls
in their youthful prime,
watching the rain,
wasting their time.

## - Acid Seas, Pebble Beaches.

They say the motherland is barren.
Her rock-cavern womb
scarred by snarling pickaxes
and bruise-knuckled dynamite.
The power stations cough
second-hand smoke
into the face of children.

The moonlight is vicious,
twisted by dark ripples
on a mirrorglass pond.
Its tundric eyes have watched
the departure of lovers,
ones dragged
through starved-hag forests
with regrets lacing their pockets.
Ones with the misery
coiled about their throats
like an ivy vine.
Like a white-knuckle fist.
Like snakeroot.

The waves
crawl up the beach
like a halfdrowned man.

What is left of my heart,
weeps for them.

## - Aeroplanes

I wonder how many of us
have wished on stars
that turned out to be aeroplanes.

## - Rain on the Power Lines

There is nothing of me here.

I am not neon,
or laughter.
No lights blaze
or flare in my night.
Just the slow drum
of rain on a dark window.

Your mechanist mind
is all cogs
and engines,
while mine
is the slow turn
of windmill sails.

We are a fox
and a housecat
with tails entwined.

You brought me here,
where you're the never ending
light of the street lamps,
the thunder-rumble
of the train line.

I am the wind
rolling over the hills
like the sighed breath
of giants.

I am the weeds
sprouting through gaps
in the pavement tiles.

I am the rain
on the power lines.

**- Watch too long and the world will show you something.**

Sitting alone
in pubs
and bars
and coffee shops.
Writing notes on life
amounting to nothing
like a polystyrene cup
with a needle-prick hole
in the bottom
being held up to the rain.

Sitting alone
in dim-lit rooms
that still hold
stale cigarettes
in jaundiced maws.

Striking a match
on brickwork
and watching the flame
gutter
       and shake
like the high-heeled
nightwalkers
down on Frog Island.

Sitting alone,
drinking coffee that's black
or whisky that's gold,
contemplating the horror
that is life.

But what a beautiful horror it is,
to live
         and breathe
and even exist at all.

## - Changing lanes at midnight with no indication

This skin crumples,
clinging to the bones that hold it
like a quivering mother's arms.
It is weak and selfish
and unapologetic for it,
just as the mind
that rattles inside
like a broken child's toy.

Beatdown in a Clio
with blood on the passenger seat
and rain trying to wash me away.
I cut the night in half
and leave rusted taillight trails
through the young motorway spray.

What a night to be alive and alone and young,
such a careless time,

                        a primal time.
The rollaway windows sleep,
sheathed in doorframe tombs,
and kamikaze droplets leap
from the somewhere dark above.

I must be the only one
with my window down
on this motorway tonight.

Mother nature is screaming.
I am smiling as the tyres
turn to rain and become light.

Sometimes I want to change the world.
Sometimes I want to kill myself.

And sometimes,

sometimes I want to drive at night,
going up and down the roads

                         and heading nowhere.

## - Striking burnt out matches

We want to burn so bright,
like a flaming star
still lighting the night,
despite the fact
it burnt itself out
and died
     years ago.

## - Rusted Sun Rays, Golden Knife Blades

The bus into Leicester
was one of the longest
I'd ever experienced.
I was weary of the world
and wary of the world
and didn't have a whole lot
going for me.

The girl next to me
had purple hair,
the colour of a winter dawn
as the sun spills itself
over the world.

I wondered if the sun
was weary
                and wary
of the world.
Or if that girl was.

I quite wanted her to love me,
but she didn't.
How could I complain?
She simply hadn't done something,
that everyone else
hadn't done.

## - Balvenie Doublewood

Citrus fruits and toffee apples,
Christmas evenings and vanilla pods.

A lattice net of single malt honey
panning for pearls of black pepper.

Like the curve of Kenny G's saxophone
and the clack of spit covered keys.

Spring water pushing its way through
an Oak Oloroso-stained sieve.

A hammerheads morning-after breath,
waking up lost in Speyside sea spray.

## - Ode to a deer carcass

Dear dead deer,
how could they
just hit you
and leave you here?

Dear dead deer,
if it would help
your troubles
like it eases mine,
I'd buy you a beer

but

dear dead deer,
I've driven past.
I no longer care.
I'm no longer there.

## - Searching for rock bottom

I think I fell
and never hit the ground.

I think I fell
into something
that burned
with the comfort
of a soft blanket.

I think I fell,
and I'm still trying
to figure out
where I've ended up.

## - An Ending

If the river that gushes
through both of us,
linking us by the dam
which we ruptured
with our hearts,
decides one day
to run itself dry,
how then shall we part?

If we find ourselves
slowly untangling
the mess of wires
that our merged minds
became over the years,
how will we know
where to cut the joins,
where one of us
was meant to end
and the other begin?

## - Falling Past Roofbeams

flooded worlds,
                    fraying seams,
buckled minds
with break
            -ing
                straps.
Worn out alleys,
                same
            old
        traps.


Taillights trail
lines of rust
down lanes
and highways.
Locomotives
charge down
the rails
of your arms.


There is little
you can now do
that would
*surprise me.*


So; s c a t t e r
our lives.


Leave
us alone,

a f l o a t
on a sea,
a vast ocean,

to flood our lungs
with the soft insistence
that this time

is the last time.
    is the last time..
        is the last time…

## - Flurries of Ash

I sit and study
the burn holes
in Gods carpet.
Clearly,
he is careless
with his cigarettes.

There is a streetlight
on the corner
that collapsed,
and when it fell
they dragged it away
like it had no soul.

The nights blaze.
Imperfect raptures
coughed
by some Chimera,
and maybe it's a thing
of mortal make,
or maybe sparks
from the Bic of Gods.

The breeze passes unseen
through the leaves.

It will carry you whispers
if you listen.

If you close your ears
to the howl of the world.

Close your ears to the jungle,
still there
                and screaming
under all this concrete.

Close your ears to all
but the whispered burn
of Gods cigarette,
crawling its way to ash
like a fuse.

But blink:

all that's left
is another average evening.

Just the beer bottles,
  the burn holes,
the Chimera,
  and the breeze.

## - An aside

(one question
is still stuck
somewhere
on my lips)
How can you let
him hold you
with anything
but reverence?

## - Open Mic

I hold my pint with the comfort of an alcoholic.
It is easier to hear my own voice if I am drunk.
It means when the words slide from my throat
they are laced with more humour than sawblades.

Dust motes swirl in the midwinter light shafts
that spring from humming bulbs,
they weave past each other like a river,
like a dance to the slow ebb of my words.

I can see you from the stage,
your eyes blooming from the dark
like algae pools.

You watch me as if I am an answer
and not just some placeholder.

I wish
                I had better poems
                to share.

**- I can't see anything wrong in there and maybe that's
what scares me**

The rooms of your skull
are all painted beige
and nothing
      in this world
will ever scare me
     as much
          as that.

## - Dreams, masks and endless eyes.

Keep those straight-laced, beige-tinted soft smiles,
how fast turn the cogs beneath such a mask?
Give me the faces flushing themselves with blood,
the ones sobbing out snotbloodtears,
the ones scrawling mascara lines down their cheeks
with a shrugging intimacy.

There is never a casual vacancy within eyes like these.
Such fools! to think that setting sprays
might hold their smiles.
These are the ones caught, self-imposed
force-feeding sadness,
swallowing it over and over in search of an end.

These are the ones wearing laughter as a shroud
while already asleep on the slab.
There are packs of black dogs running wild
through the dank streets,
spewing rabid and manic
with rolling grins and sharpened eyes.

I want to be a gentleman
but my hands are rough.
They are filled with anxieties
and never learnt to be soft.

## - I could believe that

Somewhere,
      the waves grind up
      pebbles on the beach.
They could be reaching for you,
eroding their way through land
just to try and feel your touch.

## - Fuck it.

It was a shit day.
A shit week,
shit month
year
world
fuck it.

## - Capricious

Where are they,
the halo-helmed kids
that crawl through clubs
like congenital heart failure?

We crack the sky
with the weight
of our thoughts.

A generation
all searching
for...
　　　　something
without knowing
what it is.

I can feel empty eye sockets
staring up from beneath our feet.
Their expectation burns my soles.

## - Distant fires from splintered lives

There are distant fires
reaching for star filled skies
with beckoning fingers.
I have lost myself,
wandering between the hands
of a clock face.
There is blood
smiling from concrete,
    somewhere.

Maybe I hear your name
in the wind that curls its way
down a dark alley.
Maybe the moon
will never be full again.
Maybe we can exist alone,
but maybe that's all we'll do.

**- A vigil**

Fists cracked
with brick dust
clutch tight
to paper lanterns.
Hold the vigil.

Release them.

The way you wish
you could release
all the things
that hold you down.

## - Dull-eyed dreamers

I'm stuck
in this town
where no one
has the energy
to dream.

We're all washed out.
Washed up.
Flat champagne
in a paper cup.

The bloated clouds
scud across grey sky
and our eyes
are as closed
as our minds.

## - Her

The phone chirps
like a snitch with a secret
and I see your name
scrawled
like waving papyrus leaves.

I open the chat with a single finger.

You are there,
sprawled
in a shaft of sunlight.
The cotton bedsheets,
      your pink nipples
      like licked candyfloss,
            your eyes the colour
            of deepwell moss.

My fingernails carve crescent moons.

I lock the phone,
      screen blanking like a power cut

and fall back into sleep
      to find you there as well.

## - Toothbrush

When we broke up
I sat on my bed
drinking a screwcap Bud
and forming a list
in my head
of all the things
I had just lost.

In terms of actualities
and not abstracts,
the list consisted
of just one item.
My toothbrush.

It had been a good
toothbrush.
But I guess
that at least
will be easy enough
to replace.

## - The one with the sharpest teeth

I keep looking for things
to tear apart.
Making pincushions of my head
and heart
because I've become bored
with myself.
My jagged edges are smoothing
into something
that wouldn't even cut you
if you held me with care.

## - When the torch batteries die under the covers

There is a pain in this world
so palpable
that you can hear it
in the soft rains.
The flock of birds
flying amethyst skies
as cars cut
motorway spray.
The car park streetlights
that burn with the ferocity
of a sobbing fist in a wall.

There is a pain in this world
that lives in the dull click
that cuts off torchlight,
the soft beat of a book closing,
leaving you alone
in the dark.

**- If the cities burn down, will that keep us warm?**

I wonder if you're still there,
somewhere at the corners of my dreams,
warming your hands on the fading embers
of the burnt shells of fallen cities.

## - Protein +

I have an excess
of protein
in my piss
and apparently
this means that
my kidneys
may be shutting down.

Mortality
is an interesting concept
to consider
as you walk
through the town;
especially
with a bottle of piss
warming the skin
through your pocket.

## - Opportunity Cost

I wonder what's happening
at the tops of those towers.

I wonder who's buried
within their foundations.

## - If we were streetlamps

If we were streetlamps
you'd be the one
that chose to blaze
in the middle of the day,
unafraid to outshine
the morning's flames.

## - Heartbreak Anarchy

Lavender doesn't smell
so good
when its coughing
from a fireplace.

All the love poems
I wrote for you
are now nothing more
than fuses
　　　　for Molotovs.

## - The sound of a closing door

I've been throwing mugs
against doors
and mailing my fists
through drywall.
I've been hacking
at a snare drum
and setting fires
in the street.
I've been searching
for tall trees
to cut down.
For fast cars
to crash.
I've been searching
for the sound
that coughed
from my ribcage
when my heart heard
that you were gone.

**- Keep your sunshine.**

There is no need for happiness
inside a black hole.
The cars are chasing each other
in endless circles,
the clocks frown from the wall,
but I see no reason.

I see no reason.

My hands are covered in a fluid rust,
gnawing decay seeps to fingerbones.

I wonder what skylines
are framed in your eyes tonight.

I wonder what sun is setting
to try and reach your smile.

## - I have fed him well

Love hurts and the morning hasn't even settled.
Backlit by the jaundiced sun
you hold a dented soup can
                    like a machete.

I am a frayed hardback with a slumping spine
but today I only have one broken toe.

At night the house shifts around me,
an uncomfortable shuffle at my presence.
Outside the leaves adorn themselves with dewdrops.
Rime lays across concrete in broken stanzas.

There will always be blood in the sink.
It sleeps there like rusted snowfall.

The hands of the clock are laughing as they spin,
turning with teeth bared when I reach to hold them.
I still remember how they stopped and STARED,
wide eyed gossips as I willed them to keep quiet
and turn on
                    and on
                            and on.

Those were the days when the baby monkey
was born into the hood of my sweatshirt.

## - I don't buy flowers anymore

I never understood
why cutting up beauty
should symbolise love.

Why hack down
something that burns colour
into all this grey?

Why uproot something peaceful
for another to watch
as it dies on their table,

                mantle,

                      windowsill?

What martyrdom from such frail petals.

What a mass grave,
the stained reservoir waters
of a makeshift vase.

We are worth more
than the sacrificial stems of slow rot.

Instead offer tribute of lopsided smiles,
of spiced exhalations on summer days,
of entwined legs and tear-soaked t-shirts,
of anything still throbbing from the depths
of your charred

              but still beating heart.

## - Word association

dark thoughts
dark head
cold nights
cold bed
rough days
rough sex
long lives
short deaths.

## - Riversmile

Oh Gaia,
      I love your daughter,
but the convergence
of too many deaths
has left us stacked
in battery farms.

What pockmarks we've developed.
What scabs to pick and scratch
till they scar.

Whose heart is made
of twisted metal?

*'Not mine,'* come the cries
on the sobbing nights wind,

*'Not mine.'*

## - A view from a warehouse window

The chimney is impaled
within dirt
like a Vogue cigarette.

Smoke spews from it,
meandered patterns
tugged by the breeze.

The buildings here,
seamless with grey sky.

Abandoned racking
reflects the rusted shelves
of our minds.

Fill them with something.
For Gods sake,
     fill them.

## - Anxiety

I felt your mind
like a starved bird
panicked in a cage.
Your eyes
tried to trace
the fireworks
that screamed
in your ears.

I follow the downturn
of your mouth
with my fingerprints.
Tracing there a wish
of lush grass
and skyshine.

Some days
the people
all appear
with cutout
eyeholes,
backlit
by flames.

Some days
come like
asphyxiation,
like a vacuum.

Some days
there are beasts
behind each door
and the only escape
is to crawl from your skin.

## - Observing a crash on a roundabout

There is only one bird
soaring these skies today,
between powerlines
and chimney smoke.

Taxis flash hazards
in the cold.
The old wish to be young,
and the young wish to be old.

## - I've seen it

There is a field
somewhere beyond
this articulated steel.

There are trees,
sharp-beaked eagles,
and moss that blooms.
Rivers that cut through sod
like a fist of lightning.

They are there,
                somewhere,
at the edges of my dreams,
echoing from a time
before all this concrete.

There are flowers out there.
I know,
        I've seen them.

## - Forever falling into the whaleway

the wave maidens toss their seafoam hair
as night bruises the skyline with its arrival.

Clouds press themselves against this dome of pain,
are they also wide-eyed in the face of their own reflection?

It is something we are taught to abhor.

The clumped marram grasses
sprout like knives,
cutting at our ankles till we trip.
The soil is packed loose,
aerated by our fears,
dug into soil by the jaundiced fingers
of these falling hands.

Who are we now we're lying on the floor?

The dirt covers our faces like clouds on mountaintops.
New reflections warp in the saltwaves of the ocean.

They are somehow more acceptable than before.

**- How bright will you burn when the darkness closes in?**

There is a darkness
pressing its soot fingers
on our window panes.
The constellations
of our entwined days
blaze rapture
across the sky
like a dancing horse.
The light burns
against the dead night,
a lighthouse
for those still lost
in the dark.
Some days
the embers of our souls
blaze like a supernova,
but others,
the Sun and Stars
are stuck in the sky
and we are all
stuck on the ground.

## - Hemlock

This monotone town
is weed cracked concrete
and whitewashed pain.
Cranes scar the skies
above the docks,
clawing at the birds
arcing through grey smog,
dusting their wingtips
in the exhalation of clouds.

We are stuck here
like flowers that never
managed to bloom.
We are rusted meat hammers.
We are Chelsea smiles,
serrated teeth,
dusty jars,
Hemlock.

## - Lapsang Souchong

Tastes of Fujian evenings
alight with pine bonfires.
Of fresh Lucky Strikes
and caramel Black Devils.

In Ms. Wu's tea garden
we sat, alone together.
A star shot. I pointed.

"Samolot," you shrugged
as the moon pulled
sunshine from your hair.

We drank. And evening
left tea and the unsaid
rolling over our tongues
like mist on paddy fields.

## - Syntax

I have so many things to say to you,
they spiral in my mind
like luminous dustmotes,
but the syntax of my mouth
can never compare
to the language you don't speak
with your softened lips.

## - Where wide eyes blink beneath the seas

Here I am,
haze-headed,
eyes searching
for something
    someone
    somewhere.
My brain is a hoarder.
My mind, clutterjunk full.
The world moves
in and out of focus,
    sometimes.
A strained aperture,
stretched camera lens,
or is it heat haze
from the rainbow slick
now burning
across the fields,
        the buildings,
        the clenched-teeth rocks
        and shudderhowl tarmac.
        The sighing waves.
        The forgotten bodies.

## - An Apology

My tongue has searched for words,
sliding over the calcified corpses
of everything else that died
before parting my lips.

I know they are there.
They rattle in my skull
like a half-remembered prescription
but only form themselves
from the end of my pen.

They flow now like a black cascade,
like the hair of army recruits,
like pain.

They flow like the rust stains
of my bathtub.

I am writing the words
that my lips cannot form.

**- I think I could face it, if only someone had told me.**

Why did no one tell me
how hard the pavements are,
how cold the rain?

Why did no one tell me
how long the hours of pain
that roll away before us all
like upturned carving knives?

There is beauty in a matchflame,
even as it burns the last oxygen from a room.

This world has more clenched fists
and overflowing gutters
than it would have us know.

Doors hanging limp in frames,
men with smiles that don't stretch
past padlocked lips.

I'm sure we could face it,
if only someone had told us.

## - Small sailboats over the horizon

Maybe you've forgotten me,
and maybe I'm forgetting too.
I see these words
like small sailboats
departing to the shattered
horizon.
The sun hangs
embedded in the fuzz
of velvet memories,
the same light spilling
across the alleyways
as when we fell back
into the laughing warmth
of each other.

Maybe you've forgotten me
and maybe I'm forgetting too.
The piano plays from an open balcony
somewhere in Tuscany,
the trees alight with birdsong,
the cotton drapes cinched
with old dressing gown cords.
A man fries fish in the courtyard,
seasoning the young breeze
with zest and salt. You cradle
a paperback like a child.

Maybe I've forgotten you
and maybe you're forgetting too.
These will be the last scars
my inksword makes in your name.

In the distance, the piano plays
but it is in
                 the distance.
The bright days still blaze
without you. The birds
still laugh into the sun,
and we will be captured
by another's kisses,
as we were by each other's.

## - (Artichoke Hearts)

What a bitter seed I am attempting to plant
in the cracked frost of this rutted earth.
You sit at the windowsill and fog the glass.
I break my mind in the kitchen
and fry it with an artichoke heart
but you are not hungry
and it sits,

        cooling,
on the kitchen table.

## - Gutpunched by Love, or at Least, Something

It was a grimy sea
of sighed waves
cracking knuckles
against the hull
and the Captain
had blown his brains
over the deck
like scattered leaves
and the Mates
leapt into lifeboats
screaming 'cut the ropes'
and the ship cat
shat on the kitchen floor
till an albatross
carried it off
and She was up the rigging
with the Nor'westerly
running its tongue
over her bare nipples
and a scrawny ginger Boy
lapping at her ass
like a greedy puppy
and I was still below
trying to bail out the engine room
with a rusty fork.

## - A choir in dirt

Caught in the changing of seasons,
the slow smile of a time lapse,
the soft exhalation of your breath
brushing away the sorrow on my cheek.

The world like a rolling marble,
the orchards swelling with bloated fruit
falling to sod, to oversweet in the dirt, to rot.
The worms will rejoice when we join them
and the world will laugh another turn.

Pull tight the heartstrings.
Run the bow across their being.
Stretch out our heartbreak in an orchestral wail;
one to resonate as long as we clutch tight our bones;
one to permeate the world through our footsteps,
to sink between the cracks of concrete,
        to stretch and grow beneath the flow of the world
above
so that when we die,

                    when we finally laugh and let go,
there will be something familiar down there
for us to sing.

## - Moving to a flat by the tracks

Somewhere,
        rime coats the thatch
in a sleeping village,

but here,
the streetlamp burns its glare
by my cracked window.

Trains sigh down rails,
their halogen carriages
painting neon stripes
into the cruel nights.

The rain is all
that makes this home.
I don't know what I'll do
when the clouds depart.

## - It must feel good to be unstoppable

What is it
that moves between
the pillars of your bones
like flames in distant cities?

What is it
that keeps you upright,
keeps your starlit gaze
watching the jagged horizons?

You are wildfire
laughing through
mountain streams.

You are a face
full of contradictions.

What am I,
but rusted
marram grass
sprouting,
        somewhere,

under milk wood.

## - Where's Dante?

Here
      we spin around
this nine-circled world
like pinballs.

crashinglivestogether
until they begin
to cr
      ack.

**- My heart is drunk and irresponsible, looking for love and shooting at the moon.**

Who would know
that once our minds
were almost melted into one,
like a snow sprawled landscape
of windmills and lilac fields.

Now you come as a stranger,
scratching a fingeritch
on your cold trigger,
as you push open the swing doors,
        silence the piano,
in the saloon of my mind.

Shall we shoot each other
in the town square?
The tumbleweed is prepared,
it is the only part of me
that ever looked around
        when you left.

## - When I die

I hope it is on a day like this;
the sky a clear haze in sepia,
darkening blue
swaddling the sun to rest.
Engines groan out diesel
and the grinning tramp
sells lighters outside the train station
and the birds gossip from powerlines
and the fence is collapsing,
    but no more than yesterday.

A woman cackles on a bench
and the streets are littered
with leaves and no litter
and the sink is as clean
    as fresh powdered snow,
and the people moan orgasms
behind their balcony doors
and rake each other's backs.
Surely, no one's died today,
so if that makes it my turn
then I'm okay with that.

## - Gestalt shift

A man
bound with worn rope
and dragged
across lushgrass plains
from the back of a truck
will be the first to say
there's no such thing
          as flat ground.

## - A tapestry

There are shadowed doorways
which frame moments of being.
Let us pierce Woolf's cotton wool,
let us run open fists over skin,
our own and each other's.

Who is watching through
needle eyes? The Fates
are surely not so obtrusive
as to disturb us in this place,
this finality of dreams,
this echoing atrium of valves.

We can weave something
of our own here
and know that even if everyone
tells us its ugly,

     it's still our own
and will keep us warm.

## - The cityscape

The flats are burning
in the middle-distance
and I stand on the carpark
completely prepared to jump.
For the first time in a long time
I feel my heart begin a slow thump,
and all the crows frown at my ineptitude
and the skies are bruised more than my ribs
and all the streets get longer like each passing day.

There is warmth out there,
wrapping its cloak around bodies that shudder
even as it tears down the concrete.
The gutters are full of sleeping children,
the fists clenched with knuckles bloody
and the razorblades are always too sharp
but still not sharp enough to remove you from the problem,
and you've been drinking the sorrow for so long now, it's made
submarines of your lungs
and the winding threads you hoped to mend are all coming
undone
and the pyres of lives caress the skies but the frost still sits on
your soul,
it still coats your ribcage like rime across a field
and there is a way out, somewhere,
but how do you find such a place
when you're wandering alone
and the things you carry
are chained
to your
throat?

## - Blue eyes

The greatest sparking of my synapses
is less than the slow curl of her smile,
so rafters will splinter their backs,
lightbulb filaments flame brighter,
and flowers turn from the sun to watch
her laugh, like a stream over sleigh-bells.

## - Smoke break

You're waving from the door
with no intention to return
but how will I stay warm
if I don't continue to burn
down all the things that hold me up.
So when you scream out 'fuck you,'
I can't think of anything to say but 'yup'
and I still love you too,
but hey, forget it, what the fuck.
And some days I see people
with smiles on their faces
and imagine being so happy.
Imagine being so sure of who you are
inside your own skin and head
and imagine not having that whisper
that says you should be dead
and imagine being okay,
ha ha,
imagine.

## - Barstool

I sit at the bar with a cautious smile.

The bartender has eyes like rockpool swell.

I am perfectly ready to die
and if I could tumble back
off this stool into:          ,
then I'm sure I would.

The whisky is golden
like my blood used to be
and the halogen bulbs
hum above me.

The bartender smiles,
the peach skin of her cheeks
glowing against the night.
What a titanic kindness
to offer a stranger.

The rain throws itself against the windows,
the wind tears down streets like a derailed train.

I could have watched that bartender
pull pints all night.

I could have stayed until the clock ran out,
drinking neat whisky
and watching the tides in her eyes,
until I ran out of money,
        until I ran out of days.

**- Cornwall, Wednesday, 6:47am**

Your breath on my cheek,
like the soft gust
of a butterfly
sending storms
across the world.

## - Sunrays

Her gaze on me:
like sunrays
on a ruin.

## - Fragile flames, gently blazing

Your heather
-soft whiskey-
warm honey
-slow voice
curls about
the dust
covered books
like grinning
dustmotes
in a shaft
of sunlight.

How do you
smile
with such
generosity?

How do you move:

- vases
- heirloom china
- wide eyed annecdotes
- childrens toys
- the slow change of seasons
- blankets for protection
- feelings

         from there
to here
without breaking
anything?

What cottonwool
do you contain
in your ever busy
silkworm hands?

How does it not ignite
with the wildfire
that holds you,
blazing upright?

**- Summer swinging her legs from a park bench.**

Summer was a laughing schoolchild
with grass stains dyeing greyscale clothes.
It smiled and watched you curl
a delphinium in your hair
and your thighs
b l o o m e d
from bluejean shorts.

Your laughter flowed
through the market streets
and people smiled
as you wrapped your fist
around those flowers' necks
and snap
        ped.

## - Stone fists, paper hearts

You are moving through me,
machete-hacking away at my being,

but that's okay.

Trains, too, crash through the countryside,
oblivious to the pain of the bracken.

## - The sharp pain in my shoulder screams fuck you Monday

My shoulder has ached since 4am,
the time I decided
I would stop wrestling with its
lucidity.
How can you be so worn out
at twenty-six?
Some days I forget my age
and have to count up from '94.
My old pal The Sexton Single
pats the pained shoulder
with its
shivering
touch.

I wonder if one day
I will be a skeleton wearing a top hat.
I suppose,
I can only hope.

Contour the maps.
Rake your lines along the mountain range
of the spine. Kiss the earths curvature
as it curls
around your lover's breast.

There is nothing more than this.
There is no more to come.
The cities are insomniac icebergs
sinking to the depths.

We are little and lost.

And what a way to be
what a fucking way to be
shivering,
alone,
scared of it all,
the threatening pain,
the clouds looming constant rain
but all our begging hopes
on their knees,
praying that the gutters wont spill over,
that the blood will wipe clean,
that the arthritic joints of our worn hands
will lift the spade once more.

Once it's all over
hope for a top hat.

## - Paroxetine Dreams

My brain is battered
and I am its abusive husband.
There is a caustic rot
that I keep scratching,
scarring chunks of my mind.

What would I be
without this grinning shadow
curling its inkslick fingers
around my slow-firing synapses?

I am in love with the slow breeze,
playful with the ancient trees
held upright by such proud roots.

What a gasping realisation
that I am less than I thought,
one carried by roving eyes
around the face of a clock,
the final cracking fist
in a barrage, breaking a rib,
bursting a lung like an overripe balloon.

## - The gentle winds drift between headstones

What a sweet scent
   of lilac kindness
that carries on the breeze
as you s l i d e by.

enough,

           perhaps,
for me to dig
the charred remains
of my hope
free of its shallow grave.

## - What do you wonder when the nights fall around you?

Isn't life funny?) the men ask
before the leaves turn
brittlecrisp and brown.

What a way for nature
to remind them
of the turn of their years.

Life does that sometimes,
    widens its eyes
as it drops you
    on your head.

At night I wonder,
does firewood weep
as it burns?
What is a split lip
to a blackbird's
morning-song?

The woods are dense
with the tanglebrush
of grinning thorns,
my unthinking fists
grip them
like offered hands.

There's a plastic lighter
with hope scratched
in its frowning side
that I hold
in my breast pocket.

It was full,
         once.
Now it's light
is a child's whisper.

I will hack down thorns,
uproot bramble from sod.
I will pile offerings
higher than birdsong,
throw the final sparks
onto the pyre
(and ask the only question left:

## - Negative Space

The birds wheel about the white cliffs
as if there is no one buried beneath them.
The frost
        lingers on our bones.
How are some there,
standing with locked shoulders,
squared,
staring down the riot shields
and smirking batons.

The tanks never stopped rolling through Tiananmen.
They are crossing the globe.

How are there still ones with the strength
lifting those in need onto their backs,
running the streets as if they're home;
as if the clouds of smog aren't seeping
into the spiderwebs of cracked lungs.
Ones facing clenched fists with outstretched hands.

At the bus stop there's a girl with riot-coloured eyes
and when I kissed her, she tasted like cigarettes
and bad decisions.
The schoolboys rip flowers from the earth,
the women drink,
the men leave holes in walls.
There is more meaning
in the gaps between words.
In the end,
the last of us
will be cinders and ashes
will be bones and dust.

## - Dying is fine

and a thing well practiced
within the closed parenthesis
of these cold hung arms.

The sun blistered
the tarmac of this car park,
unnoticed by commuters.

Vomit swept to a corner,
Tesco bag hostage in a tree.
Why are these things ignored
if they mean so much to me?

## - (fly now)

Look at those someones
lost alone in Tundra
or playing scrabble
against themselves
with wide-drawn smiles.
Spines like slack whips,
     once taut,
but bent under the world,
the weight of an unshared burden.

(fly now)

Concrete Mecca ant hive,
halls swamped with the smell
of dried bingo dabbers.

Here, in spacious rooms
drenched in sunpools,
the bright-tied men
and the excellent women
sit with straight backs
and knees together.
Pocket squares salute
from shoulder-pad jackets,
but what colour for their eyes?

It is impossible to tell.

Those watercolour sparks
have drained from them.

They perch in boardrooms,
swollen and overgrown mantid.

They are beasts without hearts,
committed to the worship
of slow-folded paper
and unaware
they are dead.

## - Parfum

You are a rose bush
out of bloom,

though still
entwined
with beauty,
all that really makes you
is a mass of thorns.

**- Love, sex, and other grown-up things.**

Who killed the kids
with warmth in their smiles?
Who took their bodies
and stole the small hearts
that throbbed thunder?

All that's left of us
is stretched out
on life's rack.

How can those muscles
hold onto any hope
when they work so hard
to keep these adult things
alive?

## - The Rupture

*kill yourself*

Do you ever hear
the humming streetlights
just before their bulb
   ruptures,
killing the light
housed in plastic skulls?
The words that fall
from frowning clouds
like rusted scabs.

*worthless*

do you hear them too?

the slow winds
whisper past your ears
pulling time's sand,
catching in your head.

The ants,
      the worms,                          *useless*
the parasitic germs
that crawl through the cables
of your brain
like a computer virus.              *stupid*
CtrlAltDel, CtrlAltDel

                           *ugly*

Built walls corrode
under vicious chewing,   *die*
caustic thought-teeth
of slow *kill yourself* invaders.

The world,
       the words,
*worthless* build up sometimes
until *useless* there's nothing
*stupid* else *ugly* that can
 *die* break *kill yourself* through.

## - Here, where

Here are the hands
gripping the corners
of the world.

Here the evenings
spreading over horizons
like a gentle bedsheet.

Here the hours
that fall to the floor
like tears.

Here the clouds
oppressing the ground.

Here, where the fishponds
are deeper than souls
and woodsmoke steams
at closed windows.

Here, where the world
is a tightened fist
around the gasp-lungs
homed in your ribcage.

Here the slow turn of winds
blow us between distant cities.

Here the open streets
pull us over book pages,
between bars and bedsheets.

Here with the cigarette smoke
curling from holes in sofa arms.

Dry the tears from your cheeks.

Here the jawbone curve of all life's faces.
Here the love,
          the pain,
                    the moon,
                              the rain.

## - I hope, at least

The sky is so many shades of blue,
I wonder which I can buy from Dulux.

The clouds advance,
                    rank and file,
filling my vision,

but breathe,

the sun burns them all away,
black and white,
           just the same.

It is quiet,
           and the wind pushes
the sun off my back.

Maybe they've stopped
dropping bombs
for a minute.

Maybe the sun
pushed off their riot gear.

Maybe they'll stop
           kneeling on necks.

## - Hemlock II

They see you less
because you are born
with a bloodless wound
and these are the ones
who discard as damaged
anything gouged
by the vicious edges
of the world.

They are unable to see the beauty
in reknitted skin.

Rip apart the fetters
of societal lovers.
You are a lion
made to believe
it is a housecat.
You are a claymore
being told it must live
as a butter knife.
You are a coiled snake,
a sunray splitting clouds,
a drifting eyelash.
Hemlock.

## - Now, to part

Goodbye to you
who won't remember me,
as the Parisian cobbles
forget so many lovers.
I am a stagnant leaf
within your forest
and autumn has come.

Goodbye to you
who meant so much to me,
as blue sky to a miner.
These slow-filled whisky bottles
empty themselves
as each night
is cautious when done.

Goodbye to you
who took the best of me,
the blooming grove flowers
that lace my ribs and skull.
The question you left in my head
will echo,
how can our double bed be filled
by just one?

**- I know, I do, it's just that my heart disagrees.**

How you slaughtered your lovers
comes as no shock to me
as I taste your saccharine lips.

I think I got too close to you
and saw your dreams
like spilled watercolours
pooling in the space around you,
staining into some corporeal thing.

I think I got too close
and discovered
that you are backlit by a wildfire
of a thousand colours.

The knives hung
on your bedroom door
bite into my bloodpump
as you writhe above me.

Now I sleep on the beach,
building sandcastles each evening
before the sea of your love
and hoping to call them home.

## - Architecture

There's this girl
  who glances at me
as if she doesn't know
  she's ornate;

as if she doesn't know
  someone sculpted
those cheekbones
  with Mona-Lisa-Smile
kind of care;

as if she doesn't know
I'm a dilapidated cottage
with a half-thatched roof
squatting next to the fucking
  C A T H E D R A L
that is her.

## - Architecture II

Her stained glass eyes
frame a thousand saints
that all have her face.

Her steeplestraight spine
stands as a fuck you finger
to a world beating people down.

If my eyes are blue,
hers are mushroom-clouds-in-your-
heart-atrium-the-only-fish-in-the-
rockpool green.

She acts as if
    she doesn't know
that trains carve
    down rails,
that flowers punch
    free of dirt,
and fuses struggle
    not to implode
and it's all
    for her.

## - Whitegrass

The graveyards are full
of disturbed dirt,
emptied mounds
where some claw free
of their burial-beds.
White bone fingers
wriggling from dark soil
like bloated maggots.
They pull themselves
from those deathpits.
They are the strongest ones,
though some light
will have left their eyes
and they rarely
          ever
             talk about it.

## - A (slightly) broken bike rack

The Sun is setting once again,
laughter laced in its departure.
The wind is still,

                the trees inch upward.
The bike rack squats at a jaunty angle,
its smile still echoed around
the spit-soaked streets. It whispers,
'just because you backed your car
into my spine, doesn't mean I'm too

      d a m a g e d
and need to be replaced.'


I will try to be more like that.

## - The pocketwatch

Let the clock usher in a new day,
the hands of its face pull ever tighter
on the winding thread of time.
Let us look to find a way
to pass our lives in golden rays
and speak not of all our smiling crimes.

The truth found in each moments passing
is that time is its own ouroboric assassin,
and all the wine is dying on the vine,
and all the saints stand on top
of unrecognised shoulders,
and the white maggots still writhe
around Napoleon's bones.

The eldritch winds blow through broken homes
and children scrawl upon the walls
with hopes and dreams felled low and small.

Shall I wander across the fields
where once my grandfather's reaped and sowed
and crush beneath my vicious boots
the seedlings that have not yet grown?

Times snow speckles my countenance
and drives ridges down my brow,
and all together, and all at once
the worlds ending seems closer now.

Lightbulb filaments lace through the cords of memory.
They illuminate until they break.
The breeze bypasses my uninflated lungs,
my breath still caught somewhere
between my chest
      and the upturned corners
         of your smile.

## - What fills.

There is more hatred
within the ones beside you
on the train,
or bus,
or at the next desk,
than in the eyes
of any Disney villain.

The flesh wraps around the bones
of half-remembered dreams.
We walk past the ones
sleeping in gutters
not realising they sleep
next to the revenant shades
of each of us.

The things you gave up on,
that you dropped into binbags,
grew legs and ran,
cattails whipping their ankles
and they had no home,
they'd been stamped out,
but they were free
and maybe you could have been too.

Unclench your jaw.
Unclench your fists.
Unclench the vice
                    from your heart.

## - Alchemical Reactions

The whisky gets smoother
the more I drink.

How about that.

What alchemy has created
    such wonders?
What gods filled this bottle?
    Probably the same
that made you walk
    out my
        door.

## - Highlands, 2012

My eyes were a deeper blue back then,
like a sunshaft reaching the depths of a lake,
though my smile was still crooked
and my skin covered with less of these jagged lines.

In an old cabin filled with ashsmoke and maple
we painted the greatest truths
against the bare canvas of the other,
    then we parted with smiles
that could only have been accidental,

    and I may never be sober again.

## - Evenglow

Your smile is a splinter of shrapnel
and I'm convinced I'm too young to die.

You run through the rain
like you've been chained to a drought.
Your eyes are the sleek velvet of tensed panther muscles
and I am nothing but exposed jugular.

I have stacked notebooks in piles of nothing to say.
I want to lose myself until I'm a ghost,
a silhouette on a shadow in the night,
a scorch mark on a burnt hayloft.
I want to chain myself to a promise of nothing,
nail my hands to a cross of white noise.

You stand before this confusion of wires
and tell me to tear the hook-knives from my flesh,
promising to close each wound with an apple-red kiss.

I am an origami butterfly of folded frowns being told it can
change the world
and you are singing of the storms my wings can cause.

I would swim a surging sea, split the roofbeams
of an endless succession of ballrooms
searching for the dancing green of your eyes.

I would learn to fly just to cut wide the underbellies of clouds

and bring you rainfall.

## - Wild ducks migrate in flocks

to the chalk-cliff coasts
where waves greet them
as old friends.
Winter comes around as a slow frost
coating rime on the cracked tarmac.
My fists are clenched –
as if they could hold onto the last of my good intentions.
The valley of our sorrow echoes
with the crash of love snapping,
the sound of a train derailing.
Here we are,
dancing in the whispering night,
holding tight to the rhyming sound of our blood drops,
one for sorrow,
        two for co-dependence.

## - Once I had brickdust fists

You know, Joe Calzaghe
never lost a fight
and yet, some days,
you can't even
fall out of bed.

The burly men in Spoons
chew on the rage of my youth.
It settles in their inflamed guts
and all it takes them to kill it
is a blister pack of antacids.

## - Emasculation

"Why can't you be a real man,"
her voice, as shaken baby,
"you've got no fucking balls."
I took the question
as rhetorical,
and sat in the corner
doing my historical
re-enactment of
      **me**
being ball-less and feeling
alone.

She continued to rant
and moan,
waving her arms
and gesticulating wildly.

This went on
till the point
all I could really think
was *fuck me,*
*I need a drink,*
*there should be some whiskey*
*somewhere,*
*under the sink,*
*hidden amongst the bleach.*

She must've had the same thought
because she screamed
"I'm going to the pub
and if you follow me
I'll fucking castrate you!"

I contemplated the point
of castrating a ball-less man.
She closed the door
with a slam
and funnily enough
I didn't feel quite so alone.

## - A Scottish Hamlet

"A Scottish hamlet
would be a nice place to stay,"
she says
as we lay in bed
with the autumn sun.
"We could eat oats
and drink whiskey
and sleep by the fire
as the smoke curled
from the chimney
like a beckoning finger."

"We could wrap up
in skins,
our own
and each other's,
and stay together
sharing spit
and sweat."

My father
is somewhere in Denmark
where it is cold
but a Scottish hamlet
could be warm
if we made it so.

We could dance
and drink
and float through time
like Ashrays.

A Scottish Hamlet
wouldn't send Ophelia away.
He'd fuck her raw
and put his father's ghost
down to the dram
and be all
the happier

for it.

## - Forward to Death

I was standing
outside the bus station,
watching the swell,
the cities ever-changing tide.

I slipped a Lucky Strike
from my pack
and planted it firmly
between puckered lips,
already rehearsing
the well-practiced motion
of sucking that cancer stick dry.

I lit it.

A schoolkid came up to me
and he said, "hey man,
those things will kill you."
Then he walked off
without even waiting
for my reply.
I thought to myself,
"well, you're not wrong kid."

But then again,
every time you raise
a drink to your lips
you die a little.

Every time
you tuck your kids into bed
or turn a guitars tuning peg
or get up on a stage
and read a poem
you die a little.

At least the cigarettes
are honest about it.

## - Freckles

She lies there,
sleeping,
skin like a smooth chunk
of full moon
fallen to earth.
Her shoulders,
sprinkled bits of brown sugar
slowly sinking into the cream
of her skin.

Her breathing is deep,
like a rhythmic bellows
being worked by a blacksmith.

She rises, her top
slipping from her
like some kind of
silken shroud.
My salacious fingers
dig themselves
into the peach-flesh
at the base of her back.

She turns to me,
looking over her shoulder
as she lies there
and sighs
in that beautiful
and shuddering way
that people do
when they can't help
but exhale.

## - Sunday morning

I was dreaming of the knife again when your soft breath woke
me. Your tangled hair wrapped around the mornings frosted
light. I could see your sleeping mind wandering through
happier galleries than mine so I rose //
and opened the windows, breathing deep the 6am air,
clearing the lingering scent of cigarette ash on skin.

The cold hand of winter used to purple my scars like a bruise,
now they just hum a dull red year through. The first car coughs
fumes to the frosted morning, the smell of burning petrol
reaching for my mind
            with the embers of an insistence
                    that I've moved on, that I'm no longer there.

## - The girl who saw everything

in colour was only 13
when I first met her.
Avocado eyes projected
superhuman sight
onto all passing by.

I came to school
like a dirty smudge.
Broken sole black Skechers,
knee-torn black jeans,
standard issue, uniform,
black school jumper.

But in my name she saw
so many blues it seemed
my body had its own tide.
In her mind the mundane
exploded crimson and mauve.
Colour conjured from the blank

recess' of the everyday.
A master craftswoman
hurling splashes of paint
created from single words.
Colouring backs of her retina
with a kaleidoscope palate.

Some ashen faced teacher
told me she had a problem.
Synesthesia. Maybe she does.
Though to me it seems a gift
not to see everything saturated
in so much suburban beige.

## - How do Salmon survive the seas?

I catch her
on a late Friday evening,
my line twitching
with promise.

She is gasping
and majestic
in the moonlight.

I gut her
with my fingers
and tongue,
stroking her scales
as I slip inside.

We sleep together,
the streetlight spilling
the nights secrets over us
in a roseglow tangle of warm sheets.

The morning blinks through
the depths of our rockpool.

We kiss with the finality of a trawlers noose
and find smiles scrawled on our mouths.

Her hands are velvet moonstone
as she lowers me back to the water,
my fins slick, she releases me
back to the depths of the riverbed.

## - Breathe

Breathe.
there is time
yet for you,
and if
by some chance
there is not,
then maybe
that's alright too.